Gardening Basics for Beginners

Gardening Basics for Beginners Series

Nina Greene

This book is dedicated to my Dad who taught me everything about gardening and growing my own food.

Copyright © 2014 by Speedy Publishing LLC

All rights reserved. No part of this publication may be reproduced, distributed or transmitted in any form or by any means, including photocopying, recording, or other electronic or mechanical methods, without the prior written permission of the publisher, except in the case of brief quotations embodied in critical reviews and certain other noncommercial uses permitted by copyright law. For permission requests, write to the publisher, addressed "Attention: Permissions

Coordinator," at the address below.

Speedy Publishing LLC (c) 2014
40 E. Main St., #1156
Newark, DE 19711
www.speedypublishing.co

Ordering Information:
Quantity sales; Special discounts are available on quantity purchases by corporations, associations, and others. For details, contact the "Special Sales Department" at the address above.

-- 1st edition

Manufactured in the United States of America

Table of Contents

Publisher's Notes i

Chapter 1: Introduction 1

Chapter 2: Choosing Your Gardens Location 3

Chapter 3: Prepping Your Garden Site 7

Chapter 4: Tools and Supplies 11

Chapter 5: How to Navigate a Garden Center 15

Chapter 6: How to Read a Seed Packet ... 21

Chapter 7: Seed Gardening – Indoors or Outdoors? 28

Chapter 8: How to Read a Plant Tag 33

Chapter 9: How to Choose a Healthy Plant 38

Chapter 10: How to Read a Hardiness Zone Map 42

Chapter 11: How to Read a Fertilizer Label 47

Chapter 12: How to Improve Garden Soil 53

Chapter 13: Watering Basics 59

Chapter 14: Annuals 64

Chapter 15: Perennials 68

Chapter 16: Bulbs 72

Chapter 17: Trees 76

Chapter 18: Shrubs 83

Chapter 19: Fruits and Vegetables 86

Chapter 20: Conclusion 90

Meet the Author 92

More Books by Nina Greene 94

Publisher's Notes

Disclaimer

This publication is intended to provide helpful and informative material. It is not intended to diagnose, treat, cure, or prevent any health problem or condition, nor is intended to replace the advice of a physician. No action should be taken solely on the contents of this book. Always consult your physician or qualified health-care professional on any matters regarding your health and before adopting any suggestions in this book or drawing inferences from it.

The author and publisher specifically disclaim all responsibility for any liability, loss or risk, personal or otherwise, which is incurred as a consequence, directly or indirectly, from the use or application of any contents of this book.

Any and all product names referenced within this book are the trademarks of their respective owners. None of these owners have sponsored, authorized, endorsed, or approved this book.

Always read all information provided by the manufacturers' product labels before using their products. The author and publisher are not responsible for claims made by manufacturers.

Print Edition 2014

Chapter 1: Introduction

Gardening is one of the most popular hobbies enjoyed by people around the world. Maintaining a garden, regardless of its size, is a relaxing and rewarding hobby. Gardening has been found effective in relieving stress and contributing to maintaining physical, mental and emotional health. Gardening is a productive way to spend some time outdoors and can also produce crops that provide healthy food and nourishment for you and your family.

The best advice for beginning gardeners is to start small. This will give you an opportunity to try out your green thumb. If you determine you enjoy gardening you can always expand the size of your garden. Just remember that as your garden grows so does the amount of time and work it will require.

Every single garden topic and tip would be impossible to put into one book. The goal of this book, Gardening Basics for Beginners, is to give new gardeners a very basic and general overview on how to successfully and confidently plant and grow a thriving garden.

Chapter 2: Choosing Your Gardens Location

Location, location, location! Many things in life are all about location and gardens are no exception to this rule. If your options are limited, you will have to make do and work with what you have.

The placement of a garden should be conveniently located in your yard. Gardens are more likely to be enjoyed and tended to if they are in the immediate vicinity of your house, patio, setting area, etc., and are easily accessible yet not interfering with foot traffic.

If possible, stay away from large trees that will drop leaves and may alter your soil and deplete the water and nutrients from your plants. If you are not interested in growing plants that thrive in the shade or grow vertically, such as ivy or certain vegetables, then stay at least three feet from fences or buildings. Avoid areas that have rocky soil, steep slopes, or standing water. A garden site with good drainage will reduce disease and keep your soil from becoming waterlogged which will result in your plants struggling to survive. A garden location with good soil is a plus but not crucial as soil can always be improved as we will explore in Chapter 11.

If your circumstances allow it, let the sun determine your gardens location. Your goal is to get the most sunlight distributed as evenly as possible for as long as possible throughout the day. Poorly distributed light may result in lopsided growth of your gardens plants.

A lot of plants, fruits and vegetables need at least six hours of sunlight. The ideal garden location will have southern exposure with your rows of vegetables, plants and flowers running north to south. This will give your garden the sun's warmth all morning on the eastern side and rays all afternoon on the western side.

If your garden faces southeast, run your rows northwest to southwest to get the best distribution of sunlight. Gardens with northeastern and southwestern exposure will always get an uneven amount of sun. A garden with northern exposure will have limited sunlight and may struggle depending on your choice of plants.

Most people do not have the availability of picking the "perfect" spot with the "perfect" conditions for their garden in their yard. To make the most of your garden's location will require some research on your part and maybe even some "trial and error." There are plants designed to grow in just about every climate, condition and situation. Be flexible and adapt to your gardens surroundings by finding plants that will thrive in your location and unique circumstances.

Chapter 3: Prepping Your Garden Site

For the first time gardener there is a lot of work and preparation that goes into starting a garden. Before you can start planting there are a few things that need to be planned and accomplished to ensure a successful and abundant garden.

The importance of location was covered in the last chapter. Once you have decided on the location of your garden, sketch it out on paper. Include your garden dimensions and crop or plant placement.

Next you need to decide what you want to grow in your garden. Be it fruits, vegetables, flowers, etc., you need to do some research. Knowing the needs of each plant you want to grow is essential in order for you to support their growth and keep them healthy.

So you have determined where your garden is going and what you are going to harvest in it. Your next step is to lay your garden out on the ground. This will give you a visualization on your garden's size and the spacing needed between plants/crops and walkways. Make adjustments accordingly. This step will help you estimate what you need and will save you time.

Next step is soil preparation. The area where you will be planting your garden needs to be prepped ahead of time. Debris like rocks, weeds, grass, etc. need to be cleared from the area. Till the ground to loosen it up and allow oxygen to move freely through it. Most gardeners do not start out with great soil so expect that you will more than likely need to enhance your soil to prepare it for planting. Whether your soil is hard, sandy, stony or wet, compost will improve your soil structure which will improve plant growth. Compost is good for new gardeners to use because it will not harm your garden if it is over-applied unlike organic or inorganic fertilizers that need to be used at the right time and in the right amount. Compost can be added any time, in any amount because plants will use what they need, when they need it. (Please refer to Chapter 11 for more about soil improvement and compost.)

Congratulations, with your garden site prepped you are ready to start planting!

Chapter 4: Tools and Supplies

Like all new hobbies, gardening requires some basic supplies and tools to get started. Most gardening tools can be found at your local hardware store, nursery or garden center. When starting out keep your equipment simple and to a minimum to keep your start-up cost low.

Below are suggested must have tools for the new gardener:

- Garden Gloves – Some people enjoy digging and working the soil with their bare hands but some people prefer to protect their hands and nails. Gloves provide excellent protection when tackling tasks like pruning thorny plants and are handy for other miscellaneous items around the garden.
- Garden Rake - A garden rake is helpful in smoothening and leveling a freshly tilled garden and also helps loosen soil and keep it free from weed. Rakes also come in handy when it comes to keeping your flower beds clean and free from debris.
- Shovel - The shovel of your choice can be long-handled or a short-handled one. A shovel is very useful

for digging holes, moving soils, and lifting plants.

- Garden Hoe - A garden hoe can be used to make rows for your garden. It is also useful for chopping weeds, turning over soil and for making narrow furrows when you are reaping root crops such as potatoes.
- Hand Trowel - A hand trowel looks a bit like a garden hoe with a short handle. This tool is useful for is for aerating fragile types of plants like cultivars and it also enables you to get closer to weeds to get rid of them when the need arises.
- Garden Shears - Pruning plants when there are withered or dead parts is essential to keep your plants healthy and your garden pleasing to the eyes. Fresh bouquets of flowers are just a few

snips away when garden shears are kept nearby.
- Garden Hose – Gardens and plants need water to grow strong and healthy. A garden hose is essential for transporting water and keeping your garden hydrated. A garden hose also comes in handy for cleaning dirty tools and your surroundings like pavements and sidewalks.

If you have a large area where you are planting your garden you might need to till your soil. Depending on how hard your soil is this might be a tough job to tackle. Look into renting a rototiller or consider hiring someone to do this for you.

Chapter 5: How to Navigate a Garden Center

If you are new to gardening, your local garden center, nursery, farm center, plant center, etc. may be an unexplored, foreign territory for you. The following simple tips will arm you with a strategy to make your first visit, and every visit, to your local garden center a simple and successful shopping experience.

Before you step foot into a garden center as a "buyer" you need to have done some preliminary homework and planning. The design of your garden and planting scheme decisions need to be made in your backyard and not in the nursery while purchasing plants.

Part of planning includes making a list for your garden shopping excursion. A list for your garden needs will keep you focused and within your budget. Needed items will not be forgotten and impulse items will not be purchased. Make your list as specific as possible and account for factors such as sun verses shade, etc. The more specific your list is, the easier it will be for staff to assist you.

If you are unsure about a section of your garden or a specific plant, bring along pictures of the space you are going to plant in and consult the nursery's staff. Ask questions and put some trust in the staff members experience and expertise.

Upon your arrival at the garden center, always grab a cart or nursery wagon as you walk in. You will need it to hold the multiple items you will be purchasing and it indicates to the staff that you are a serious buyer verses a browser.

Be polite and friendly to the employees and staff. It is more than likely you will making regular trips to your favorite local garden center so you want the staff to look forward to helping and visiting with you.

People who work at garden centers do so because they enjoy gardening and planting. These people are usually full of experience and knowledge, and truly want to help you accomplish your garden projects. Take advantage of the free knowledge and advice these people have to offer by asking questions or simply asking for help. Consider shopping during the week when business is slow and staff members will have more time to spend with you.

Finally, just because you have a list of needs and maybe some wants, does not mean you should not be on the prowl for deals. You should always scan sale items, check out the clearance racks, and look for bags that are torn or ripped.

Sale Items – Garden centers are no different than any other retail store in regards to something always being on sale. After you arrive and grab your cart and do a quick survey of new items on sale. Stay focused and only purchase sale items that you need or can use.

Clearance Items – Great deals can be found in this section. Unlike retail stores selling other types of items, garden centers deal with living products that are constantly moving through different stages of their life cycle. Other reasons why plants end up on the clearance rack may be because they do not look as fresh as they once did, overstock, or maybe the plant just is not selling well.

Torn or Ripped Bags – Garden centers often order and sell large quantities of fertilizer, soil, grass seed, etc. It is inevitable, from handling or over time that bags tear and rip. Instead of throwing out the contents they are often repackaged and sold at discounted prices. If you need compost, fertilizer, grass seed, or any other bagged products, look around. If you do not see what you are looking for do not hesitate to ask. Employees may have an item that they have not had time to repackage and put out but would be happy to get rid of and sell to you.

CHAPTER 6: HOW TO READ A SEED PACKET

So you have decided to cultivate and grow your garden from seeds. Before you get started you need to understand the information on the seed packet and how to use it. Seed packets contain symbols, abbreviations and pictures. The look of seed packets will differ from one distributor to another. If you purchase quality seeds you will find everything you need to know for the success of growing that particular plant on the seed packet. Useful information and tips are found on the front, back and inside of the seed packet.

Front of the Seed Packet

- Name – The common name of the seed and usually the Latin name of the seed inside the envelope. It is not uncommon for plants to have the same common name therefore the Latin name can help you determine if you have the seeds you want.
- Picture – An image of what the seed will look like in bloom or harvest.
- Weight – The weight of the seeds contained in the packet.

- Seed Description – A description of the seeds contained in the packet such as "Vegetable" or "Annual."
- Price – The price of the seed packet is usually in the upper right hand corner.
- Light Requirements – Full sun, part sun, morning sun only, etc.
- Bloom Time – When the plant will most likely bloom.
- Height – How tall the plant will be when it blooms.
- Description – Some history on why this seed variety is interesting.
- Seed Company – The seed company name is usually located at the bottom of the packet.

Back of the Seed Packet

The back of the seed packet is where most of the information about your seeds is contained. Follow the information and advice to be successful in starting and maintaining your plants.

- Name – Again the type of seeds that are contained in the packet.
- Catalog or Inventory Number – Commonly in the upper portion of the packet will be a catalog or inventory number.
- Description – Details and characteristics about the plant or vegetable, when to harvest, how many feet it will sow, etc.
- Planting Chart – The chart will tell you how many days it takes for the seeds to germinate, how many days after germination until ready to harvest, how deep in the soil the seed should be planted, how far to

space seeds apart, how many plants need to be thinned or removed, etc.
- Suggestions Section — Not all packets have this but if they do, read it.
- Planting Zone Map — A table and chart that tells you the best times of year to sow the seeds for the area you live in. (More about zones in Chapter 9.)
- More Plant Information — This can be cultural, anecdotal or historical information.
- When to Sow — When to start your seeds for both indoors and out.
- Special Germination Instructions — Any special instructions exclusive to that seed.
- Last Frost — The average date when a particular area no longer

experiences freezing temperatures in the spring.
- First Frost – The average date when a particular area experiences their first freezing temperature in the fall or winter.
- Expiration Date – A "sell by" date, an expiration date and a lot number.
- Seed Company – The company information such as address, website address and usually a help number.

Some seed packets utilize the inside of the packet for some of the above information so get into the habit of taking a peek inside. The information and its location will vary from each company. It does not take long to familiarize yourself with seed packets and quickly find what you are looking for.

Always be sure to check the expiration date on packets because fresh seeds will give you the best results. It is also recommended that you write down the dates on which you sow seeds so you do not have to rely on your memory and no guess work is required. Online gardening journals are also fun and handy to track your gardens progress.

Chapter 7: Seed Gardening – Indoors or Outdoors?

As a new gardener the time will come to decide if you are going to create your garden from seeds, ready-to-plant species, or both. Buying a packet of seeds is a fraction of what ready-to-plant vegetable starts and flowering plants cost. Another benefit to working with seeds is a larger selection of flowers, vegetables and plant varieties that may not be available in your local garden center.

Healthy and vigorous plants, trees, blooms, fruits and vegetables all get their start as seeds. Plant seeds need to be started in warm, moist soil and this is called germination. The germination process causes the seed to come out of dormancy and produce a plant. Sunlight is not needed to start this process but lighting (natural or artificial) will be necessary for the growth of the plant. Seeds can be planted and nurtured indoors or outdoors but seasoned gardeners know the best way to get a jump on the growing season is to start their seeds indoors. Seeds are easier to start indoors verses outdoors because the perfect grow conditions can be created and controlled year around.

Plants that are started indoors will need to be prepared for outdoor survival before transplanting them. This process is called "hardening off" and is a gradual introduction to sun, wind and temperature changes to avoid shock.

If you choose to start your seeds outdoors (direct seeding) you need to consider the growing requirements of the seeds you plan to purchase and harvest.

- How much daily sun do your seeds require?
- How warm does the soil need to be?
- How much space will each plant need when mature?
- What is the best time of year or season to plant your seeds?

The advantage of direct seeding is for plants and crops that are known to struggle if transplanted from one location to another.

For beginners it is recommended to start off outdoors with seeds that germinate quickly and are easy to grow. Vegetables and annual flowers fall into this category.

Whatever your reason for growing plants from seeds the process is not very difficult. Whether you choose to harvest seeds indoors or outdoors avoid the following mistakes new gardeners make with seeds:

- Not reading the directions on the packet and following the instructions.
- Investing in seed starting equipment before you have

determined whether or not you enjoy planting with seeds and will continue.

- Not using quality organic soil or potting soil. Never use garden soil because it may contain disease or organisms that can kill young seedlings.
- Overwatering or under watering.

It is recommended you start with just a few seed packets on your first few attempts of harvesting seeds. This will prevent you from becoming overwhelmed yet still give you an idea of the process involved with planting and growing seeds.

Chapter 8: How to Read a Plant Tag

Plant selection is a fun part of planning and implementing a home garden. A new gardener can quickly become intimidated and unsure by their lack of knowledge about plant varieties, colors, care, growth, etc. No experience is no reason to become overwhelmed before you even get started. Everything you need to select the perfect plant is on the plant tag.

Plant tags come in different shapes and sizes but all include basic information. A good plant tag will tell you everything you need to know to care for the plant and include a picture of the plant as it will appear at maturity.

The front of the tag typically has a color photograph and lists the plant's common name, scientific names, sun, soil, and water requirements, hardiness zones, and size information. The back of the tag may have details on transplanting and caring for the plant, which is crucial to the survival of some plants such as perennials, shrubs and trees.

Four Things you need to look for, and understand, on a plant tag before making a purchase:

    1. Plant Description – The plant description will give you details

about the plant: if the plant flowers, the color of the flowers, if the plant keeps its leaves (evergreen) or loses its leaves (deciduous), if it has a fragrance, what the fragrance is, etc.

2. Growth – Look for information on how tall and wide the plant will get. The tag should also give you the plant's growth rate: fast, medium, or slow growing.

3. Care Requirements – When you are picking out plants, it is important to know how much sun and water a plant requires. Look for descriptions such as "shade," "part shade," "full sun," and part sun for sun/light requirements; and phrases like "keep evenly moist," "needs moist soil," or "drought tolerant," for water needs.

4. Hardiness - The United States is divided into eleven different planting or "hardiness" zones. Each zone is 10 degrees F warmer or colder in the winter than the adjacent zone. This information is important to have because you do not want to purchase a plant intended for a cold and snowy Zone 3 when you live in a warmer, tropical Zone 11. Look for instructions on the tag such as "Hardy to Zone 5" or "Plant in Zones 8–9." You can use Google to find out what zone you reside in. If you are unsure or confused about zones and hardiness, ask your garden center expert for assistance.

Take the time to examine plant tags. The details and facts crammed onto the small plastic tags are provided for your benefit. Plant tags are helpful resources to assist you with growing and nurturing your plants.

Chapter 9: How to Choose a Healthy Plant

As a garden hobbyist it is important to become knowledgeable on how to choose a healthy plant. Some plants can carry harmful diseases that could cause it to die within a few days after buying it from your local nursery or garden center. Worse, it could be a carrier of disease and pests and infect your other plants.

This is why gardeners need to become educated on how to choose healthy plants for purchasing and planting.

Leaves and Structure

When learning how to choose a healthy plant, the first thing to consider is the leaves. Thriving plants usually have multiple stems with thick foliage. The leaves need to be green, shiny and spread out to absorb the sun. Height is not necessarily a contributing factor since it may indicate that the plant is stressed from capturing the sun. In most cases, a plant that is unusually tall will have a spindly main track and will be easily breakable.

Roots and Stem

Take note of the roots especially if the plant is potted. Ideally the roots will be well entrenched in the soil, providing a firm grip. Avoid plants that have roots growing out of the pot because this can be an indicator that the plant is stressed. Also pass on a plant with few roots since this indicates the plant has been recently planted and needs more time to become established. As for the stem, simply check for cracks, chips or scratches on the surface.

Diseases

Most plant diseases can typically be found on the surface of the leaf area. Carefully inspect this part of the plant, watching out for discolorations or white flecks under the leaf area. Holes and black spots are also indicators of unhealthy plants.

Flowers

If you intend to purchase flowering plants, do not buy one that is already in full bloom. Look for plants that have tightly formed buds so they can bloom after you get them home. Buds also have better chances of being transplanted than those that are already in full bloom.

Buying a healthy plant provides the best chances of transplanting them, but even sick plants can be saved with a little TLC.

Chapter 10: How to Read a Hardiness Zone Map

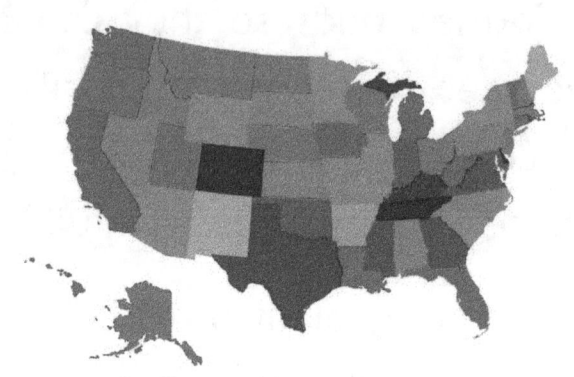

A hardiness zone map (also referred to as a planting zone map) is a good source of information of climate data. All gardeners should look at planting zones when in the beginning planning stages of a garden.

Planting zones are a guide to plants survival rate ability during the coldest winter months in a particular region. If a plant can survive the winter climate, it can successfully move into the next season.

When cold weather arrives, many plants will go dormant. Dormancy is a good thing for plants that are cold hardy. For plants that are not, they will not survive being exposed to the chilly, frost-bitten, lower temperatures. Therefore, gardeners need to be aware of how low temperatures can drop in the region they live in.

Choosing the right fruits, flowers, plants, trees and vegetables in the right planting zones is essential to successful gardening. Double check that your local garden center and/or nursery is stocking plants that are compatible with the gardening zone they are sold in. If purchasing bulbs, seeds and seedling online or through catalogs, they should be tagged to let gardeners know what zones they are best suited for.

The U.S. Department of Agriculture's (USDA) gardening zone map represents the average annual lowest winter temperature experienced in each region or "zone" throughout the United States, Mexico, and Canada. The map divides North America into 11 separate zones with zone 1, Alaska, being the coldest and zone 11, Hawaii, the warmest.

Map zones 2 to 9 are subdivided into two sections. Each section (a&b) represents a 5 degree Fahrenheit difference in each zone with the lighter shade being colder. Alaska and Florida are examples of states that fall into multiple zones. Florida starts at zone 8b and ends at 10b.

The U.S. Department of Agriculture released a new hardiness zone map on January 25, 2012. The map had not been updated since 1990 and the new version accounts for variables that affect plant survival such as terrain, elevation, exposure, and proximity to water.

The new USDA map is available online at http://planthardiness.ars.usda.gov and is interactive. The interactive map lets users click on their exact location and get detailed starting dates for planting.

Gardeners need to remember that a hardiness zone map is only a guide. There are a ton of other stressful factors, such as air pollution and below average rainfall for your area, humidity, an odd timed cold snap, the amount of frost or snow on the ground, and soil moisture which can affect the performance and/or survival of a plant.

Click on the above link and enter your Zip Code or your State for your zone information.

If you reside outside the United States, Google can help you locate your plant hardiness zone map.

Chapter 11: How to Read a Fertilizer Label

As a new gardener it is important to absorb how fertilizer can benefit your garden and how to utilize it. A trip to your local garden center to check out the available fertilizers can leave you very confused. Different bags will have different cryptic numbers and it will quickly become apparent that fertilizer is not created equally. An important step in caring for your garden is learning how to read a fertilizer label correctly and understand it.

Good fertilizer is an important part of gardening as it supplies plants with supplemental minerals and nutrients to boost health and growth. Plants essentially need three nutrients in order to grow and be healthy; nitrogen, phosphorous, and potassium.

Nitrogen (N) – "Healthy Plant Growth"

- Enhances stem and leaf growth.
- Gives grass and other plants a rich green color.
- The most important nutrient for a lot of plants.

- Too much nitrogen can make plants susceptible to pests and diseases.

Phosphorous (P) – "The Plant Energizer"

- Encourages and strengthens plant and root growth.
- Encourages the development of flowers, fruits and seeds.
- Improves a plants capability to absorb water and nutrients
- Assists against environmental stresses

Potassium (K) – "The Immune System Regulator"

- Assists in warding off pests and plant diseases.
- Increases root growth and assists with overall health.
- Increases size and quality of plants.
- Improves drought resistance.

These three nutrients work together to give your plants growth and a strong immune system.

Commercial fertilizer bags are identified with three numbers separated by hyphens that are usually printed in large bold characters on the front or the back of the bag. These numbers refer to the percentage of the three important nutrients that are present in the fertilizer and are listed in order as numbers on the package (N-P-K). The first number represents just how much nitrogen there is in the fertilizer. The next number is the amount of phosphorous, and the last number is potassium. You will notice that fertilizer's recommended for lawns are nitrogen heavy and will have a high first number. An example of a balanced fertilizer is 5-10-5 (5 percent nitrogen, 10 percent phosphate and 5 percent potassium) or even 5-10-10. For a new gardener who is trying to promote plant growth, an all-purpose fertilizer with more phosphorous than nitrogen is commonly recommended.

Take a look at the rest of the packaging and you will find the other nutrients that are in the fertilizer, like iron and calcium, which are also important for the growth and health of your plants. Usage instructions and recommendations will also be found on the bag. For instance, if the fertilizer is water soluble then it that means you must dissolve it in water before feeding it to your plants.

Once you understand the basics of reading a fertilizer label, you will find the appropriate type of fertilizer to give your plants and ensure their health and

abundant growth.

Chapter 12: How to Improve Garden Soil

To grow healthy plants in your garden you need quality soil. A good garden soil is deep, loose, fertile, well drained and has decayed organic matter. This ideal soil is rarely available challenging gardeners to improve upon what you already have. You might not be able to completely change the texture of your soil but there are some tricks to make it better and allow for healthier and larger plants. You must be patient as it will take some time and effort to actually improve your garden soil, see visible effects and get results.

There are three basic soil types:

- Light Soil
- Heavy Soil
- Loam Soil

<u>Light Soil</u> - Light soil is somewhat sandy or contains silt. It has large particles, is usually light in color and feels coarse when wet or dry. Keeping in moisture and nutrients can be difficult with this type of soil and you will need to feed and water your plants frequently.

<u>Heavy Soil</u> - Heavy soil is made up mostly of clay and is not ideal for plants and gardens to grow in. It is very slippery when wet but very hard when dry. This

soil does hold water but its soil particles are too close together making it hard for roots to penetrate and water to drain. Puddles are often present in heavy soils.

<u>Loam Soil</u> - Loam soil is a mix between light and heavy soil making it ideal for healthy plants and gardens. It is composed of rather coarse or large particles which make it suitable for good drainage and permeability. Loam soil also has finer particles, including organic materials or clay, in order to keep in nutrients, moisture and fertility.

In order to improve your soil you must first determine what kind of soil you have in order to make necessary adjustments. The most commonly recommended way to improve light and heavy garden soil is with organic materials.

The negatives of both light and heavy soil types can both be improved by adding organic matter. Fine clay particles found in light soils can be physically separated by course organic material. Nutrient and water holding qualities of heavy soil can be increased as organic matter breaks down, and the compost ingredients have soil improving characteristics.

Combine about 2 to 3 inches of organic materials 6 to 8 inches deep on the topmost layer of your cultivated garden bed to boost its composition. This layer will decompose and approximately two more inches should be added each year. Heavy soils will take two to three years before an improvement will be noticeable.

Organic materials can include leaves, bark, sawdust, wood shavings, Peat moss, grass clippings, vegetable matter and even animal wastes (manure). These materials decompose and release nutrients ideal for healthy plant growth.

Heavy soils can benefit from a 2 inch layer of sand in addition to the organic matter. It will help your garden soil with high clay content. If sand is applied without the organic matter you run the risk of creating low grade concrete with the fine clay particles acting as cement.

Adding fertilizer to lousy soil may be tempting but is not recommended. Over the long term, your soil texture will never improve and your plants will never really be healthy. It is better to increase the organic matter in your soil and fertilize your plants as needed.

Improving garden soil is an important process that does not occur overnight. Be consistent in treating your soil but you must also be patient to reap results.

Chapter 13: Watering Basics

In order for your garden to thrive you need to learn how to correctly water your plants.

How important is water? At least 90 percent of every plant is composed of water. Without water plants wilt and die but too much water is just as bad as not enough. If plants or their roots are repeatedly submerged in water they may drown or rot from the lack of oxygen.

Be knowledgeable about the water needs and growth stage of the plants in your garden. Young plants and seedlings need more water in warmer weather as opposed to older more established plants. Fruits and vegetables that are maturing will also need more water in order for them to produce more. An inch of water per week (rain plus irrigation) is the standard recommendation for most gardens and plants.

Deep, infrequent watering is recommended for established plants. Deep watering encourages deeper rooting which leads to stronger, healthier plants. Shallow, frequent watering tends to result in shallow root systems and high water loss through evaporation. Shallow watering wastes a lot of water and does not meet the needs of your plants.

Pick a watering device that matches the needs of your garden and the time you have available to water. Once a device is selected, know the correct way to use that device in order to water efficiently.

Root feeders are effective for watering trees and shrubs if used properly. The root feeder should be used away from the trunk to be effective because roots that take in water are not near the trunk. A tree or shrub's root system will usually be in the upper 12 to 18 inches of soil so do not make the mistake of placing the feeder too deep into the ground.

Soaker hoses are effective for watering vegetable gardens and flowerbeds. They allow water to seep out consistently over the entire length of the hose. Water goes right to the root system and very little water is lost to evaporation. Another benefit to using soaker hoses is reducing the risk of disease because leaves stay dry and are not exposed to water.

The ideal time of day to water is early morning before the temperature heats up. This gives your plants a water supply and prepares them to face the heat of the day. If watering cannot be accomplished in the morning then early evening is the next best option. Be sure to water early enough in the evening so leaves have time to dry before nightfall. This will help your plants avoid the development of fungal diseases.

Regardless of the watering method you choose or the time of day you water, provide your plants with enough water to keep the soil moist for optimal health. Be aware of possible restrictions in your area when it comes to water usage for lawn and gardens.

Chapter 14: Annuals

In the colorful world of gardening, the term "annuals" refer to plants that can only live for one gardening year. Even though annuals can only live for a short time, they do bloom into the most colorful and vibrant flowers and produce lots of seeds that can be used to plant in spring the following year.

How to Select Annuals

Like other plants and flowers, annuals can be found in your local garden centers and nurseries. Annuals can be purchased as seeds or as plants that already have flowers and those that have not bloomed yet. If you are an avid gardener or a confident beginner, choose the plants that have not bloomed. It is a lot of fun and much more satisfying to see your annuals bloom in your own garden.

If you buy annuals as seeds there is an important thing you need to remember: the seeds must be given enough time to germinate, grow, and ultimately blossom. Annuals purchased as seeds must be planted early in the spring.

Helpful Tips for Taking Care of Your Annuals

Growing annuals from seeds is rather easy. They do not need much attention once they have been planted. Just be sure they are planted in quality soil and they get plenty of water in warm/hot weather.

For beginning gardeners it is easier to plant annuals directly in the garden rather than in indoor plant containers or windowsills. If you start planting the seeds in early spring just as the ground starts to warm up, annuals can practically grow by themselves. There are also self-seeding annuals that sow their own seeds before the start of winter and even if left untouched will germinate by themselves the following spring.

Annuals planted near a tree(s) in your garden will need constant watering because trees tend to absorb a lot of moisture from the soil.

Though they only live for just a year, annuals help brighten up any garden. Avid gardeners look forward to spring and the process of planting new annuals which once in full bloom will provide color for the season and new seeds for the following spring.

Chapter 15: Perennials

Perennials are plants that live for two years or more. Most flowering perennials bloom during the spring or summer months and then seem to die just before autumn, only to reappear the next year during spring. Unlike annuals and biennials, perennials do not have to get re-planted every year.

Perennials have such long life cycles because they have underground reproductive structures much like tubers and bulbs. Perennials go dormant when cold weather arrives and they begin re-growing when the ground begins to grow warmer. Perennials whose foliage or leaves die out and re-grow the following year are called Deciduous Perennials. Perennials that keep their foliage all year round are called Evergreens.

How to Choose Perennials

When choosing perennials to plant in your garden, you need to first check that they can actually grow and thrive in your location. The best way to make sure that the plants you choose can actually survive in your location and climate is to buy them from your local garden center or plant nursery.

There are a few perennials that can bloom even during the winter months;

consider purchasing some of these if you want to enjoy your garden even during the colder parts of the year.

When inspecting perennials in a garden center, carefully look at the plant crown; this is the area around the base of the plant where the plant shoots emerge from the soil. Look for any signs of rotting or wilting. This will mostly ensure that the plant will survive after you transplant it into your garden.

Tips on Caring for Your Perennials

Do not over-fertilize sun-loving perennials (those that do well in direct sunlight rather than in the shade) this will only cause them to grow taller. If perennials get too tall they will become top-heavy and fall over.

You should "pinch" your perennials early in the springtime. Pinching means taking the tips off from the plant stems by using pruning shears or by using your fingernails (hence the term pinching), to make them grow bushier and sturdier. By pinching early in the season you can give your perennials enough time before winter to grow stronger.

No garden is ever complete without at least two or three perennials. These plants are a staple and a "must" if you want to enjoy your garden the whole year round.

Chapter 16: Bulbs

What is a bulb? A bulb is essentially a plant that has a short stem or leaf base. These plants are quite robust and bring color into your garden year after year unlike annuals that have a short lifespan. The reason behind bulbs' rather long lifespan is all thanks to its leaf bases, which ironically does not grow any leaves, but it does have a lot of scales which contains all of the nutrients that the plant needs to survive harsh weather conditions that can kill most other types of plants.

How to Choose Bulbs

Looking for good bulbs to plant in your garden is basically the same as looking for good onions in the supermarket, mainly because onions are a type of bulb. Look to purchase bulbs that are firm to the touch and avoid any with soft spots or discoloration.

A two-headed bulb means that it will yield two blooms. Buy these if you can unless you are looking to plant tulips because only one-headed tulip bulbs bloom.

You should into consideration the space available in your yard when out buying bulbs, for there are some bulbs that require a bit of space in between them to grow and produce bulbils (the bulb's "seeds").

Tips on Caring for Your Bulbs

Give your bulbs some space. Bulbs that do not bloom may be too crowded. If bulbs get too clumped together they will not grow and produce flowers. If this occurs the best thing to do is dig some of them up to provide proper spacing.

Long-stemmed bulbs like lilies need to be cut off the stems fairly close to the ground before autumn arrives; this will prevent the onset of stem rot that can kill the plant.

When digging up bulbs it is better to do it when the soil is dry so they are not saturated in mud when pulled from the ground.

Bulbs require more care and maintenance as compared with other flowering plants. However, the extra bit of work is rewarded with colorful blooms for many, many years.

Chapter 17: Trees

Trees are the biggest and longest lived creature on earth. They can give your garden shade, texture and its framework. Trees also provide more beauty for less effort than any other plants. Gardening with trees is more sustainable than having large areas of grass and annuals.

There are numerous benefits to having trees in your garden. They can offer natural shade, they filter the air, provide privacy, add value to your property, make your garden feel more complete and lastly they are good for the environment.

How to Select a Tree

You will need to decide what kind of look, style or theme you want in your garden. It is important to remember large trees are best suited for large gardens. You will also need to consider what trees will do well in your climate, how much sun your garden gets, whether you want to accomplish more color or shade for your garden, how fast a tree grows, a trees size at maturity, and how messy a tree is. Ex: flowering trees are pretty but messy when they lose their flowers.

A few well-placed trees in a garden can look amazing, while too many trees can become overpowering. Once your planted trees have become established they will require very little maintenance and will bring beauty to your property and garden for many years to come.

How to Plant a Tree

To improve a tree's chance of survival it is very important to choose a good location and learn how to properly plant a tree.

Dig Hole

Dig a hole that is approximately two or three feet wider than the ball of your tree. (If your tree's ball is 2 feet wide, dig the hole 4 or 5 feet wide.) If your dirt is hard or clay like, dig your hole at least twice as wide as the ball of your tree.

Tree roots will have a more difficult time moving through harder soil at a young age. Dig your hole a little deeper around the edges leaving the center of your hole higher where your tree's root ball will sit. This prevents the root ball from "drowning" because it is continuously sitting in water. Instead, excess water will flow to the deeper edges of the hole and the roots can drink from the edges if needed.

Your holes depth should be about the same depth as the container (wire cage or wire root basket) of the tree, or just deep enough so that the base of where the tree comes out is slightly higher, ½ to ¼ inch higher, than the ground around it. This will prevent water from pooling next to the trunk base which can cause the tree to rot.

The soil level of the tree in the container should be level with the ground after you fill in the hole. Do not over bury or leave any roots exposed.

Take Care of the Root Ball

Avoid handling or moving your tree with the burlap off. Remove the container from the root ball and place your tree into the raised center of your freshly dug hole. Straighten your tree using dirt on the side the tree is leaning. Next you need to remove the burlap by cutting it off as low on the root ball as possible. Remove any rope to prevent "choking" as the tree grows. The container and burlap need to be removed from the root ball so the growth of the tree's roots do not become restricted as the tree ages and grows.

To prevent a tree's roots from drying out and becoming damaged, do not leave out of their container or burlap for very long. It is best to transfer from the container and burlap into the whole immediately.

Fertilize, Compost and Water

If you are using commercial fertilizer, less is more. Too much commercial fertilizer can make a tree less likely to do well over the long run. Use approximately one handful for small trees and two handfuls for large trees. Evenly sprinkle the fertilizer around the root ball and backfill the hole with dirt. If you have access to compost, backfill your tree's hole with one third compost and two thirds dirt.

Once your new tree is planted give it a generous amount of water, allow settling, backfill with more dirt and add more water. This will help to eliminate air pockets. Water approximately one gallon for every six inches of tree height.

You need to ensure that you allow ample soil space per tree to allow them to grow healthily and reach full maturity.

CHAPTER 18: SHRUBS

Shrubs, also referred to as bushes, are woody plants with low branches close to the ground and smaller in size than trees. Shrubs often have more than one stem and these are called canes. Shrubs can be found with varied leaf designs and in a variety of colors. Shrubs are grown and cared for very similar to trees.

Planting shrubs does differ slightly from planting trees. Shrubs should ideally be planted in the spring, giving them a long stretch of time to get established and acclimated. In areas where the temperature is fairly constant year round this is less of a concern and shrubs can be safely planted in the fall or winter.

When planting, it is important to maintain moisture in the roots of the shrub. Water them as soon as possible after bringing them home, mulch and shade them from sun after their initial planting. Water your new shrubs well in the fall before the ground freezes in areas that have cold winters.

Pruning is necessary with shrubs and most shrubs need to be pruned yearly. Remove older branches even though they may not have anything wrong with them. Pruning will keep your shrubs young, healthy and prevent problems before they happen.

Shrubs can be used to cover bare patches of ground, used as boundary markers or as a privacy screen. They have great decorative appeal and are commonly grouped with other shrubs or with perennials and colorful annuals. Shrubs add color, shape and variety to any garden or yard and are a perfect backdrop for flower beds.

Shrubs provide good foliage, make a garden look populated, complete and are virtually hassle free. No excessive attention is required to have a garden that is as beautiful as a well-tended, nurtured one.

Chapter 19: Fruits and Vegetables

There are many wonderful benefits to a home garden. Growing fresh produce right in your own backyard and brought directly into your own kitchen can be a heady experience as well as cost effective. With a few basic tips there are many fruits and vegetables that lend themselves to being successfully cultivated and cared for by the beginner gardener.

All plants need three basic things to thrive: water, sunlight, and nutrients from the soil. If any one of these three items are lacking, the odds of your garden surviving are very slim. It is important to choose a location for your garden that gets plenty of sunlight but also gets some shade at the hottest time of the day. Your crops will also need plenty of water and especially during summer months when the soil tends to absorb moisture quickly.

Properly preparing the soil for your fruits and vegetables is one of the most important components to a bountiful garden. In most cases, raw soil does not have enough nutrients in it to keep your crops well nourished. The better you prepare your soil before planting, the more successful your garden will be. Do not overlook fertilizing your plants regularly to be sure that they are getting enough nourishment.

You need to be aware that insect pests, weeds, wild animals and family pets are all out to destroy your garden. Pests such as beetles, aphids, spider mites, plant lice, horn worms, the vegetable weevil and other small insects want to munch on your plants and if not deterred, will destroy your garden. Commercial and low toxicity pesticides can control pests but alternative methods also work without the use of chemicals. A few alternative methods to control pests are; barriers and traps, can trap, collars, netting, sticky board, beneficial insects, diversified planting, crop rotation, and companion planting.

Vigilantly scan for weeds in and around your garden. Weeds are competition for the same space and nutrients that your crops need for growth. When weeds appear pull them out immediately. Unfortunately there is no permanent way to keep weeds out of your garden besides physically removing them after their arrival.

Lastly, rodents, birds, squirrels, deer, cats, and the family dog, etc. will greedily and appreciatively sample your garden if access is easily granted to them. Proactively protect the fruits of your labor with mesh, fencing, netting, scarecrows, owl decoys, reflective tape, mirrors, herbs, etc.

Tending a garden takes some effort but the payoff for the any level gardener can be delicious.

Chapter 20: Conclusion

Gardens evolve and change and are a continuous process as seasons change and something new is always happening. As a gardener you will grow and discover what works, what you like, figure out better ways to do things and learn from fellow gardeners. The best gardens are never finished and should reflect the gardener's personal taste and flair. Finish up your research, choose a garden style or design you like, get dirty and have

some fun.

MEET THE AUTHOR

Nina Greene grew up a country kid in the foothills of Northern California and acquired her love for the outdoors, gardening and landscaping from her father. Forty-plus years later, Nina still resides in Nor Cal and tends to her organic garden that provides fresh fruit, vegetables and herbs for family, friends, neighbors, co-workers and occasional wildlife. Nina's *"Gardening Basics for Beginners Series"* is designed to help future garden enthusiasts get their hands dirty without feeling overwhelmed.

MORE BOOKS BY NINA GREENE

Garden Styles: Introduction to 25 Garden Styles

Vertical Gardening: More Garden in Less Space

www.ingramcontent.com/pod-product-compliance
Lightning Source LLC
LaVergne TN
LVHW021943060526
838200LV00042B/1909